LM 1059976 2

D1437912

SANCTUARIES

CHRONICLES OF SOLITARY WANDERINGS

SANCTUARIES

CHRONICLES OF SOLITARY WANDERINGS

SELECTED POEMS

RICHARD ENGLAND

midseaBOOKS

LIBRÌA

SANCTUARIES

CHRONICLES OF SOLITARY WANDERINGS

S E L E C T E D   P O E M S
RICHARD ENGLAND

EDITORIAL COORDINATION
Antonio Carbone
Antonio Graziadei

GRAPHIC DESIGN
Maria Teresa Quinto

COVER+DRAWINGS
Richard England

PRINTING
Grafiche Finiguerra
Lavello Italy

PUBLISHERS
Casa Editrice Libria
Melfi Italy
libria@interfree.it

Midsea Books ltd
Malta
sales@midseabooks.com

First Edition December 2006

ISBN 88-87202-80-X

FOR
RICHARD ENGLAND
FROM
JOHN HEJDUK

POET TO POET

11/17/98

I am very touched by your collection of poems ... the poems are beautiful, haunting,
mysterious and precise ... I have read them over many times ... it's the soundings of
the depths and the understanding of life.

Thank you.

John Hejduk

SANCTUARIES

Brian J. Dendle

I discovered the poetry of Richard England fortuitously—or should we perhaps say providentially? since the discovery led ultimately to a visit to Malta and a renewal of an undergraduate friendship with Fr Peter Serracino Inglott, the former rector of the University of Malta and also my godfather—in 1996 in the check-out line of a French supermarket in St Nazaire. A bearded stranger, Rémy Begouen, introduced himself and sought my aid in the French translation of *Island*. Rémy Begouen had spent time in Malta—he describes his Maltese adventures in *Une Perle Noire* (St Nazaire, 1988). I do not know if Rémy Begouen ever published his translation of *Island*. I myself was entranced by the poem. I journeyed to Malta in 1997, where I met and was deeply impressed by Richard England with his talents as internationally-renowned architect, theoretician of "sacred space", skilled draughtsman of imaginary "dream-scapes", poet, and music-lover, a "neo-Renaissance man", as he has been dubbed by the architectural critic Mario Pisani.

I was deeply flattered and honoured when Richard England invited me to write an introduction to his most recent collection of poems, *Sanctuaries*, although I fear I cannot do full justice to such a rich and varied selection. I have already discussed in greater detail than this brief Introduction permits the poems of *White is White* (1972), *Island: A Poem for Seeing* (1980) and *Gozo Island of Oblivion* (1997) in "Richard England, Poet of Malta and the Middle Sea", *Scripta Mediterranea* 18 (1997): 87-105. I refer the reader in search of further information to this earlier study.

In his introductory poem "Dance of Dialogues", Richard England announces certain themes of the collection Sanctuaries: time, solitude, dream, mystery, "rapture and despair". Poems 16 to 37, "As I Search the Ground" to "This Holy Earth", reproduce poems previously published in *Island* and *Eye to I*. In stately, almost prose-like verse (although a powerfully-accented syllabic stress in each line reminds us that we are dealing with poetry, not prose), Richard England offers a vision of the Maltese Islands seen in a context of eternity, outside of historic time. England addresses themes of galactic time, early religion, cosmic awe, loneliness, spirals (a feature of Maltese Neolithic sculpture), cycles (of women's fertility, of recurring time, of lives), of annihilation (the legendary creation of Filfla, "Legend of a Fallen City"; the lost continent of Atlantis, "Psalm for Atlantis"). Neolithic religious practices are evoked in references to temples, tombs, worship of goddesses and of the "Cosmic Mother", "subterranean cults of wisdom", oracles, sacrifice, prayer, ancient rites, sacred stones. England's verse in these poems is emphatic, reflecting its religious nature (in *Island* the poems were printed in upper-case letters), with frequent alliteration (a way of connecting by sound disparate elements in the universe) and use of noun plus adjective combinations rather than finite verbs (again suggesting an incantation to cosmic forces). Going beyond the evocation of a pagan, prehistoric Malta, one glimpses the possibility of Christian redemption: the longing for "a child of peace" and "brotherhood of man" ("Psalm for Atlantis"), and a plea that "[Man] may find once more his peace / and learn to love again" ("Stones Standing in Silence").

The following cycle of poems evokes happy memories of Richard England's childhood visits to Gozo (from 39 "Calypso's Isle" to 49 "The Winter of This Life"); these poems are more intimate and lack the cosmic dimensions of the *Island* poems. "Calypso's Isle" presents the Gozo landscape in deeply sensual terms rare in England's work: "its naked hill-top breasts / deep lush valley thighs / and sultry buttock curves..." "Għawdex" is a loving litany of names of Gozo villages, linked by "bulbous church dome breasts" that attest "an island's faith". "Gozo" is a joyful evocation of colour. "Dwejra" links a shared fishermen's meal with Christ's miracle of the Feeding of the Five Thousand on the shores of Galilee. "The Legend of San Dimitri" tenderly narrates a tale of simple faith. Other poems in the Gozo series contrast the joyful memories of youth with the loneliness of present "relics of remembrance".

The following cycle of poems (58 "In the Moondance of Eventide" to 93 "Come Walk with Me") treats the theme of death or, rather, of death mingled with the separation from the loved one. Certain poems ("In the Moondance of Eventide", "At the Moment of My Death", "In Dream I Feared the End", "Over the Reddening Theme of Life") offer hope of resurrection or at least of a new dawn. Many poems treat sombre themes of ageing, impending death, decay, oblivion. "Tranced Sleepwalker" offers a terrifying fear of extinction: "I tranced sleepwalker / with sails no longer full / steer a battered empty hull / down poisoned paths of doom. / A lonesome shipwreck of amnesia / on a never ending journey to extinction". Other poems, on loss of love, separation, loneliness, are tenderly heartfelt. Occasionally, England shows a certain exaggerated Romantic morbidity, eg., "I wanderer of love / perched on the ladders of legend / drink from the goblet of incest / and / taste the chalice of death" ("Angel of the Dark").

The next series of poems (from 94 "Why?" to 107 "On This Side of the Poem") defies overall classification. My own response to this group of poems was immediate; they are sheer delight. Conversational, witty, often brief, they express profound truths in terms of simple wonder and recall the light, imaginative forms (or "nonsense" poetry) of verse supposedly intended for children. Poem 107 ("On This Side of the Poem") is a gem worthy of inclusion in any anthology of modern verse written in English. Longer poems on mythological themes (113 "Thira", 128 "Klepsydra" and 129 "Euphonia") are impeccably crafted and have a lightness of touch that contrasts with the grand-iloquent tones of the *Island* poems.

A deeply-felt Christian faith dominates the six poems ("Paradise", "Cain", "Angel", "In Companionship of Loneliness", "The Lord is There to Take his Hand", "I am the Resurrection"), impressive in their dignity, humility, and simple affirmation of Catholic belief.

The final poems of *Chronicles of Solitary Wanderings* treat a variety of topics: awe at the splendour of God's creation ("Sunflower", "Rainbow"); a Romantic questioning of the poet's task as seeker of wisdom ("The Beginning of What I am", "Invitation to a Dream", "The Poem Remains"); the horrifying néant of atheism when seen in the context of eternity ("The Atheist Creed": "eternal centuries of nothingness ... an endless absence of time"); the intimately auto-biographical ("The Unwritten Poem"); themes of dream, loneliness, the passage and paradoxes of time; the deeply-felt evocation of Mary's contemplation of Christ's passion ("All This Had to Pass"); the passage into eternity ("Past the Portals of Paradise", "And We Awake in Paradise"). The final poem of the collection ("We Shall Have Met and Loved Again") is a hauntingly-beautiful affirmation of love and eternal life.

Sanctuaries impresses the reader with its diversity of themes and levels. There is a Romantic side to Richard England, evident not only in the powerful cosmic invocations of the *Island* poems, but also in the anguished cries of the tormented lover facing death, solitude or the absence of the loved one. Another side of Richard England is gentler, playful, tender, whimsical, imaginative in a sense that would appeal to the dreams of a child or adolescent. In poems of simple but deeply-felt piety, of light narrative, of "nonsensical" (but, in fact, profound) questioning, of affirmation of love, of fantasy (as in the evocation of imaginary cities that remind one of the "dreamscapes", England's exquisitely-crafted drawings of distorted buildings that appear to emerge from fairy-tale or medieval romance), there emerges a somewhat shyer poet of genuine talent. Despite the richness of his vocabulary and the variety of his cultural references (such as his evocations of the imaginary cities of Voe and Eudoxia), *Sanctuaries* is well within the comprehension of the educated reader. Indeed, England has no fear of juxtaposing the modern and the past, as in his reference to "coded e-mails etched in stone" ("In Latent Temple Walls"). Richard England's verse flows freely and always with dignity, while avoiding the too easy cadences of the popular poet. Above all, Richard England combines words in phrases, which in sheer imaginative power and concision take the breath away, the spirit of true "poesy": "Verses carved / east of the moon / west of the sun / on a shoreless sea / midway between / the chemistry of dream / and the alloy of reality" ("Dance of Dialogues"); "Stranger on Earth / moonbound in a soundless sea" ("Stranger on Earth").

The relationship between one art form and another has been much debated by theoreticians. The following considerations by Richard England on his poetry are relevant: "I suppose the architect in me considers poetry as building with words, a form of sculpture in sound. The making of a relationship of sound, silence, rhythm and melody is a paramount consideration as is also the creation of a strong imagery and in-depth meaning, all expressed with a controlled feeling. I am particularly interested in the flow, cadence and incantation of the chosen vocabulary, i. e., how the word crafting works phonologically. Perhaps one is searching for a muse of magic, music and feeling that has the capacity to carry the reader away. The sounds, tones and semi tones, or what I would like to term the taste of words, must be balanced by the modulations of the intervening silences, which are of course as important as the sounds themselves. Also, I believe that the words must dance not only aurally but also visually". (Communication of 15 November 2005)

It has been a privilege to introduce *Sanctuaries*.

SANCTUARIES

DANCE OF DIALOGUES

Fearful of time's consuming path
on roads of endless solitudes
these lines of light and darkness
fall heavily at my feet
words difficult to release
yet impossible to retain
thoughts unquestioned and unanswered
umbilical choreographies balanced between now and never.

Chronicles of solitary wanderings
on drifting stage-sets of the mind
transient images from a shadowed land
scenarios in the reflective waters of my life.

Verses carved
east of the moon
west of the sun
on a shoreless sea
midway between
the chemistry of dream
and the alloy of reality.

This secret script
reflects a child of change
in mirrored moods of rapture and despair
thematic themes emitted from the soul
a dance of dialogues in private consultation
with the reverberating oracle of my hidden inner self.

AS I SEARCH THE GROUND

As I search the ground
for traces of my ancestors
to decipher messages
of dead millennial stones
day's last sun rays
dye the sea a blood red tint
and
birds take off a sea-borne carrier base
carve poems in the mist
braille-like tactile graphic lines
for modern man to read.

On reddened soil
a white skeleton of ochred stone
icon of a timeless god
weaves spiral patterns in the wind
while high above from cracked echoes in the sky
a silver pathway bathes the sea
from land to isle.

In a dream I took your hand
and yearned to walk along this road
this thread of light
to galaxies beyond our time
where death exists no more.

In the Middle Sea
under an eternity of stars
two continents meet
oscillating
between remembrance and desire.

Island cast in my prayers
island shaped in my fantasy
island fashioned in my thoughts.

Glacial waters fill your mind
earth's blood flows in your veins
limestone marrow sets your bones.

Yesterday's target
blueprint for tomorrow
island of promise.

I hear your voice
I hear your call
I hear your plea.

Narcissist bride of the waters
sigh and pine your endless languish
maiden of vanity
let me cradle your sorrow
monadic mistress of solitude
reach out and take my hand.

Stranger on Earth
moonbound in a soundless sea.

Menstrual tides from sleeping goddesses
stain sterile waiting waters
in a trance of death
a dormant island dreams
its cracks and fissures
cradle fertile seeds of ancient gods
undetonated ecstasies of illicit love.

Unconceived
aborted
still born.

Iceberg of stone
melting in a burning sea.

Island carved in spiral dreams
sentenced to death by drowning
descend to underwater gentleness
no more to be sired by rays of the sun
no longer to be nourished by breasts of the Earth.

An eroding fossil on the seabed
cradled forever by lapping waters.

Lamented
inanimate
deceased.

As ancient standing sacred stones
bear silent witness from afar
time fulfills the oracle.

Temple stones
megaliths of truth
metaphors of memory
where man once prayed
and
worshipped the goddess of this land.

Today these solstice markers
still chant their sacred psalms
prayers of ancient wisdom
passed to modern man
paragons paradigms
for the congenial reconciliation
of
nature and mankind.

LEGEND OF A FALLEN CITY

Ancient Island
prisoner of eternity
carnal relic of a fallen city
tamed by layers of centuries
a traveller returned from forbidden thresholds of desire.

Although you belong to one time and I to another
I see and contemplate in veiled oscillating light
visions of sleep-walking maidens on bone-grained shores
washed by dripping tears of water-coloured skies
illicit dreams from death's eternal sleep.

The legend says that when a city died
this isle was born
under a waning sky of sorrow
its siren song remains unsung
quiescent music hushed to muted silence.

On some days I am sure I hear in a far and distant murmur
as the sea forever breaks its waves against this rock
the sound of voices crying in a never-ending chant of death.

PSALM FOR ATLANTIS

Relic of ancient wisdom
vestige of a lost continent
fossil impregnated with knowledge
rise phoenix-like today
refresh once more this world with love
that we may again produce
a child of peace appropriate to our times.

Show us the expectant waves of hope
in lights of beauty and belief
help us walk with heads held high
the road which takes us to our promised land
where we shall dwell for years to come
in tranquil co-existence with our brotherhood of man.

ISLAND

Island
war
shelter
birds nesting

Combat ranges
men fall
crosses rise

Island
peace
haven
target practice

Flak
volley
salvo

Island
carnage
tomb
the birds have gone.

And waves caress dismembered limestone bones
as a floating carcass marks death's eternal time.

On this Island of solitary giants
from the darkness of the Earth
subterranean cults of wisdom
mould curves compressed in masonry
singing stones dancing in the solstices
litanies forged in numerical harmony.

The people of this clairvoyant isle
in allegiance to their land
cast amalgams human and divine
metaphysical symbols of unity
umbilical dyads of fertility and sterility
where death meets birth in cycles of return.

Sea
Rock
Island

Cavern   Maiden   Seer
Tomb   Woman   Sage
Temple   Goddess   Medium

Sign
Omen
Oracle

Seed   Birth   Corpse
Plant   Life   Burial
Crop   Death   Re-Birth

Tide
Time
Cycle

Line   Day   Earth
Circle   Month   Moon
Spiral   Season   Sun

Planet
Cosmos
Universe

ENCHANTED ISLE

Enchanted isle
a traveling pilgrim's shrine
at the crossroads of the Middle Sea
temple for the Goddess of the Earth
oracle of the mantic moon
where sarsen stones of silence
mark thresholds of land and sky
necropolis of hope
lifegiver to the dead.

In the fertile currents of this rock
as woman's mysteries flow in blood
altars of double spirals
carve symbols of time returned
channels of ritual healing
in clairvoyant slumber
a priestess sleeps in trance
in this land of the Cosmic Mother
wisdom comes in dreams.

THE PEOPLE OF THIS LAND

On this land
solitary shrines of womanhood
curves without origin
arcs with absent ends
enrich man's ever-searching soul
map the meaning of his life
guide him to his everlasting time.

On this rock
in the bowels of a sacred earth
the people of this land
voyagers in a cyclic spiral dance
die in order to be born again
and in between their many lives
think only of return.

IN LATENT TEMPLE WALLS

On a floating isle in latent temple walls
lurking lines of tangram themes
emerge from nescient adumbration
coded e-mails etched in stone
a primal poetry from the past
revived for modern man.

The secrets of this nascent law
reveal once more today
man's ancient wisdom of respect
for nature's ambience and its rules
his love and kinship for his kind
his canon rite of peace.

Now in this world of evil and despair
these weathered words of wisdom
unfold once more their treasured texts
to illume the darkness of our time.

As the moon rises to take possession of the night
I walk this temple of knowledge
hear its sapient voices chant
mournful lamentations
evaporating across a now lost and famished land.

Antiphons of sorrow
canticles of melancholy
of
the Goddess of this Place
returned today
knowing no one
and
no one knowing her.

AS EVENING FALLS

As evening falls
the strumming melodies of silence
bleed the red remains of day
a darkness pure as black
engulfs the silent temple walls
stones withered and cracked with age
splash against a leaden sky
sentinels of knowledge from the past.

Goddess of the pale-faced moon
transparent walk your silver dreams
embroidered by the stars
bless these people and their earth
mould and carve in limestone bones
their transient destiny of life
and as hours turn to years in time
the womb of life fulfills the oracle.

The fragrance of the vibrant dawn
heralds the fleeting clouds of Spring
solitudes of floating whiteness
lace the darkness of the skies
heal the sterile scars of Winter
paint the land a golden tint
as the sleeping stones of darkness
awake to the fertile landscapes of tomorrow.

The people of this clairvoyant isle
in allegiance to their creed
carve cyclic curves on spiral slabs
amalgams sacred and divine
cite morning rites with twilight hymns
fragrant fugues and choral chants
oratories to the goddess of the land.

And as the maiden sun rays
of this natal dawn of spring
mark daybreak's clock-time dances
on vernal temple stones
barren seeds and shrivelled plants
to verdant crops return
in radiant reborn melodies of nature's rhythmic role.

Stones standing in silence
enclosures for the mother of fertility
metaphors searching for the substance of eternity.

Altar
shrine
sanctuary.

Petrified music in rhythmical spirals
masculine symbols in feminine curves
cardinal instants in the evolving path of man.

Oracle
mandala
temple.

Precursors of Pythagoras
mergers of science and art
observatories to mark the movements of this Earth.

Sun-dial
time-piece
calendar.

I ask you goddess of this land
where has all this knowledge gone
denuded in the dance of destiny
buried in the sands of time.

I pray you Mother of this isle
from your cosmic tomb of never ending curves
washed in the primeval blood of sacrificial earth
exalted by the mystic knowledge in your veins.

Awake these stones once more today
from their tranquil sleep of death
restore the secret of their cults
and embrace again their vast galactic plan.

Ask them that they return anew to man
his harmonious presence in this World
that he may find once more his peace
and learn to love again.

Yesterday
we walked hand in hand
across time's long-worn tracks
where once a temple stood
of lines curving into secret circles
and man knelt in prayer
your hands and mine
reached across the waters
to caress an outcast rock
icon of solitude
altar of sacrifice
crucified against the sky
in a sea devoid of logic
an island burned but not consumed.

Today
I sit and watch
a lonely island rock
awaiting your return
in hypnotic trance
midway between waking and sleeping
in petrified vision and ossified dream
I hold the hand of absence.

Goddess of the Middle Sea
long before you reached
the shore lines of this land
science-fiction movies
shown in Altamira caves
foretold the legend of this isle.

Standing stones and spiral shapes
triad temples tangram tombs
secret archives of galactic lore.

Sentinels of sagacity
wardens of wisdom
keepers of knowledge.

Daughters of the burning wheat
rainbow lit and poppy tranced
heed the omen of the oracle
war-like strangers from afar
poisoned winds and blackened skies
will raid and wreck your radiant realm
erase the sapience of unarchived wealth
and stunt for ever more in time
this mantled chrysalis of peace.

Where man once trod and toiled
and paved a paradisal path
now only faded truths remain
unwoven tapestries threads unspun
scatalogical sepulchres in clandestine corridors
lost in the subliminal calandars of unrecorded time.

THIS HOLY EARTH

I tread these ancient time-worn tracks
memorials to the syntax of this land
to probe the molten silence of this place
and sense its pulse-beat in the air
the call of man's ancestral dreams
haunts the shelter of these stones
while shrivelled leaves from borrowed skies
fall beneath the voids of emptiness.

I walk the darkened alleys
of this place called loneliness
through stabbed realities
of once sacred dreams
breathing sounds of sorrow.
In this lot of time
not the passage of years
nor death can hush this place.

I sit in this shadowed garden
a body scattered in wounded fragments
singing canticles of mourning
in cemeteries of evening twilights
my path marked by fear
in frozen wastelands of desire
I seek to find a reason
for man's self-inflicted death.

I kneel and touch this holy earth
to feel its fertile throbbing force
chant a muted sacred prayer
that the spirits of this place
may once again attain
their long-lost custody of this land
recall the ancient rites of old
in a stillness of all sound removed.

I stand timeless
in calendared reference of yesterdays
and will a potent sleep.
My dreaming spirit turns
wraps a silver mantle round my world
lights up the eclipse of this life
dreamscapes in landscapes
from somewhere back in time.

I trace this temple's winding paths
coiled in web-like spiral shapes
while echo-messages from these stones
see me through the darkness of these years
work the colours of my life
carve alchemies in my changing bones
and guide me through the walls of time
where death exists no more.

CALYPSO'S ISLE

On lapping waves
a rocking boat
towards an island steers
hills squared
houses cubed
churches curved.

A floating rock
in times before
temptress to all these
earth's temple shrine
Calypso's home
fortress of the Cross

Today its naked hill-top breasts
deep lush valley thighs
and sultry buttock curves
in smoking sun-burnt dance
still erotically allure
the traveller of today

OGYGIA

On
OGYGIA
as
CALYPSO
enticed
tempted
and
seduced
ODYSSEUS
slept and dreamt of Ithaca

GĦAWDEX

Through Mġarr
Għajnsielem
Qala
and Nadur

To Xagħra
Rabat
Kerċem
and Munxar

Past Għarb
Għasri
Xewkija
and Sannat

From all of these bulbous church dome breasts arise
nourishment of a peoples' creed
testimony to an Island's faith.

DWEJRA

As we descend a winding path
faces tinged and nostrils teased
we approach the wave lapped shores
of an inland cliff lined sea.

Summer is all pervasive
insects drone the air
in the frenzy of nature's resurgence
we share an incandescent scene.

A group of salted fishermen
from incoming boats descend
to land the profit of their toil.

In the shade of their boat house wall
the embers of an open fire
roast sampled species from the catch.

A gesture of the hand invites us to partake
the eldest of the group signs the cross of Christ
breaks the bread and shares the fish.

I know now that on that day
we shared the miracle of a meal
not there and with a few
but back in time with many more
on the shores of Galilee.

GOZO

Carts orange
donkeys brown
women black.

Tomatoes red
peppers green
melons yellow.

Seas blue
skies indigo
churches purple.

Streets ochre
salt-pans silver
sunsets gold.

And I, in the technicolour of these spectrumed scenes
once danced overdosed in the ecstasy of youth.

The legend says
that when the son
was taken by pirates of the sea
the mother wept and prayed
within the cliff-edge chapel walls
and as she shed her painful tears
the painted saint on horse-back
from gilded frame emerged
galloped over wave and surf
to return
with rescued prisoner by his side.

The mother knelt in thanks
and vowed to daily light
the silver oil-lamp of the shrine
till death did end her years of life.

For long her promise she did keep
till violent storm and quake
dislodged the chapel from its site
and crashed it to the sea.

The passing years had hushed the tale
then divers delved the darkened depths
of now calm waters tamed in time
a spectral vision caught their eye.

Beneath the azure sea
in weathered stones
and silent fissured walls
the chapel stood erect.

Entering through its rusty door
they viewed the portrayed saint
in worn and weathered frame
proudly guarding aisle and nave.

And on the ashlar altar stone
the silver oil lamp still alight
fulfilling in the sands of time
a pious mother's loving vow.

CITADEL

In the empty silence
of this gold stone town
I walk chastened and forlorn
tracing wounded patterns of despair
stenciled outlines of dejection
while above in the mirror of an anguished sky
the waning moon freezes in its burning light.

On this dark road
as white shadows further chill the night
only absence fills this space
time fades into past memories
and I retrace my search in vain
for the illusive prism of black light
to illuminate the sadness of my life.

My music has lost its sound
the song surrendered to silence
burnt in ashes of moon-raked grief
a fallen rainbow from the vaults of heaven
in scattered fragments of frigid acid greys
forgotten constellations chisilled into oblivion
melancholy illusions of once coloured joys.

As night gently turns to day
and the sun's alphabet unfolds
a magic flame illuminates the dawn
the walls blaze anew in golden ochre tones
a vision to restore my faith
and my soul awakens resplendent in belief
sometimes I think I am alone in worshipping this town.

THE GHOSTS HAVE GONE

I remember those nights well
as the moon rose silently
to greet the evening light
I paced the tortuous pathways
of this ancient hilltop town.

As I mapped its shadowed secrets
I swear I shared my strides
with phantom spectral shapes.

And in the slivered mirrors
of those mellowed moon-lit stones
we even spoke at times.

Today alas the ghosts have gone
they are no longer there
and as the town church clock hands
meet to etch the mark of midnight
I walk these streets alone.

Two score years ago
I traced the silent walls
of this stone lined ancient town
and lived the spaces of this house
shared its laughter in my heart
in youth's ecstatic time.

Today I stand forlorn
closed outside the cobwebbed doors
my fingers trace its furrowed forms
aged by transient tides
textured fissures in the walls
unmasked readings from the past

A date inscribed
an emblem scratched
a name engraved.

Markings of adolescence
frozen files of memory
recollections of a faded past.

A lost traveller on life's mapless road
offspring of lamented yesterdays
now chants the pains of distance
in orphaned companionship of loneliness
silent incantations twilight texts
atonal music scored in absent tones.

A tear rolls down and cleans away the dust
decoding ancient marks
relics of remembrance.

And as the hour glass of life
further sheds its grains of sand
this wandering pilgrim
once more is made aware
that the winter of this life
descends too soon ahead of time.

YOUTH SLIPS AWAY

As the moon
inevitably
and
in
silence
traverses the night sky
inescapably
and
in
melancholy
youth slips away.

I CALL YOUTH'S NAME

With tamarisk voice
in arsenals of sorrow
I call youth's name
spelling the chemistry of its sound
in echoed dialogue
on the flattened nipples of these hills.

Where are you now?

In butter coloured fields
sun freckles of a dancing sun
light the dark divorces of my life
between the holding of our hands
distanced by the calling of the wind
only memories now remain.

A TANTRIC KOAN OF WISDOM
HWA OM SAH

On a hidden hill-top plane
veiled in penumbras of grey
silent and secluded
a Buddhist temple stands
a place of prayer a house of peace
where time stands still and seems here not to pass.

In this meditative stillness of solitude
perched on a pagoda platform
a moon-viewing monk chants his sutras
evoking a silence of nought.

This ancient Asian shrine
remains to this day
transported in time
a tantric koan of wisdom.

I walk the criss-crossed patterns
of the cart-ruts of my land
ask their furrowed fractals
to unravel and reveal
the scratched and savant secrets
of their hieroglyphic scripts.

In quiescent trance transmuted
I soar in astral flight
then from this cosmic viewpoint
these enigmatic markings
reveal their latent codes.

Pointers passwords thresholds doorways
star gates to our world
satellite semaphores
lithographic guidelines for visitors from space
astronomical instrumentations for galactic navigation.

Intersecting incantations
interlacing initiations
xylographs glyptographs
annotated scores of amity
for remote and distant worlds.

Celestial path markers cosmic peace makers
earth's abacus for aliens
where once past and future merged
and
time echoed eternity.

I DREAM THIS HOUSE
I

I remember well the red draped room
a chamber not too often used
in secret once I sneaked inside
and roamed its cluttered paths
of chests and closets chiffoniers
candelabras chandeliers
and portraits hanging everywhere.

There I sensed a gelid stare
propelled from florid frame
of a laced ancestral dame
and as I raced away in haste
hawk-eyed she trailed my path
and with a piercing gaze
laid bare my very soul.

I DREAM THIS HOUSE
II

And as once more I dream this house
I cannot but recall
a large capacious cupboard
of burly bulk and stalwart size
behind its black and heavy doors
endless shelves and hidden drawers
a closet of secret dreams
a temple in the house
a family's chronicled narrative.

In youth I longed to peer inside
and read its muted scores
aubades of love and fugues of hate
passion pleasure fire pain
but time has taught me many things
and now I know
that the illicit stories of this chest
are better left untold.

I DREAM THIS HOUSE
III

As once again I dream this house
I recall those rock-hewn stairs
descending to the nowhere of the dark
my infant mind assured
that in that cellar demons lurked
with bandits brigands buccaneers
imprisoned maidens convicts slaves
chained in vaults with padlocked doors.

Its access I'd detour
conditioned and convinced
that this dark and cryptic cell
was best left unexplored.

THE UNWRITTEN SHRINE

I visit this place built by no one
this house of the listening walls
where the sphinx of the night is awakened
and the past is buried and burned.

I trace its saltmines of mystery
through the blood on the crest of its waves
there I etch my own patterns of sorrow
congealed in the closets of time
on the walls of the unwritten shrine.

In the moondance of eventide
I see the tombstones crumble
the dead arise from their sleep
angels mounted on stallions
overcoming the power of death.

PHANTOMS BREAK THEIR TOMBSTONES

Escaping from the grave
phantoms break their tombstones
flee their field of death
evaporated cadavers
released from mortal bondage
rise in celebratory redemption
and
in harmonies of deliverance
chant
anthems of release.

AT THE MOMENT OF MY DEATH

At the moment of my death
earth will take my body
heaven greet my soul
my life sentence served
I shall forever be released
from the prison of this life.

DO I CONSUME TIME

Do I consume time?
or
does time consume me?

In the meantime
spoilt for choice
death awaits
and
marks its time.

As my memory scans its long-lost past
in the no-shadowed time of childhood
I search the ashes of an ardent life
that once flamed my flesh of youth
this fertile blood of ecstasy
now turned to frozen foam
silenced cries cast in sterile sadness.

Rising from this wounded sea
in grey-walled harrowed grief
burned and withered in age
I recognize a face I have not seen before
its wrinkled scornful mouth
breathes a bitter kiss of welcome
and I taste the salt of Death's wanting lips.

I GAZE ON THE VISAGE OF DEATH

Past the cloistered retreat of this sanctuary
I walk the graveyard of doom
from its walls of gelid aversion
susurrant sounds of sorrow
congeal and chill my bones
canticles of anguish
from
the voices of the dead.

Mantras of melancholy
to
mesmerize my mind.

Then as these mendacious melodies
evanesce and fade
from the opaque mirror of the abyss of the damned
a shadowed semblance secretes to sight
and
I gaze on the visage of death.

THE SPHINX OF TIME

The sphinx of time looks me in the eyes
reflects the mirror of my tangled mind
scattered fragments of a shadowed past.

Life is but a process of decay
the search more precious than the find
and as I conclude my given time
death comes and takes me in her arms
where I shall rest in the endless silence of oblivion.

I can no longer reach you
since you passed away
still I hold your number
in my contacts list
and
I keep on calling
in ever yearning hope
that from the realm of afterlife
you will return my call
then once more shall I rejoice
at your sentient voice
which alas I hear no more.

IT RAINED BLOOD

On the day
the souls of the suicides wept
it rained blood
stained the earth
and
impregnated man
with the unacceptability of death.

TRANCED SLEEPWALKER

In the autumn of a pewtered life
through faded mirrored eyes
I search the xanthin hues of youth.

Spin cobwebbed brittle threads
wrinkled crevices of shrivelled time
past tortuous passaged years.

As silent windmills stilled by age
carve wanting winds of vacant voids
lonely clocks with absent hands
strike hours of endless midnights.

From a broken suitcase of oblivion
I unpack lost fossil thoughts
tangled tapestries from the loom of life.
sable sunsets of aborted dreams

I tranced sleepwalker
with sails no longer full
steer a battered empty hull
down poisoned paths of doom.

A lonesome shipwreck of amnesia
on a never ending journey to extinction

IN DREAM I FEARED THE END

In a room seemingly without walls
its only light the shadows in between
a phantom gothic window frame
I lay myself to rest and sleep
and dream a theme of death.

At the dawn of this spectral scene
I awake only to perceive in fear
that death is waiting at my side
to take me in her wanting arms
and lead me to the land beyond recall.

Yet while in dream I feared the end
now open-eyed I know it's but a dawn
and I launch myself convinced
that death is not a final act
but a natal threshold and a birth
to a richer life beyond
in a never-ending world
far richer than our own.

WHEN I DIE

When I die
place my carcass
on this rock
stretched along the cleft horizon of its spine
bare flesh on burning earth
tossed by vibrant winds
exposed to salted air
washed by timeless waves
a naked sacrifice in mournful cadence of compassion
under the magnitude of endless skies
in a silence that deepens time
to sleep my final sleep of death.

When I die
place my body
on this isle
gulls to pluck my rotting flesh
pitted bones and vacant skull
outlast and drain their given time.

In the penumbra of death
island rock and human bone
merge into a waxen limestone whole.

Under a crepuscular sky
as each midnight haunts a mute catafalque of death
this floating grave
becomes
my astral passport to eternity.

ANGEL OF THE DARK

Soul of the night
angel of the dark
my eyes bleed passion
on the carved geometries of your body
I dream galactic sex
the sunbird of ecstasy flies over our bodies entwined
in the midnight of a moonless sky
I dance in step with the Pleiades
all is a seductive chimera
and
I wanderer of love
perched on the ladders of legend
drink from the goblet of incest
and
taste the chalice of death.

YOUR LAST FAREWELL TO ME

Since my coffin holds no opening
I am unable to behold
your last farewell to me
but as you pass my body
I draw you in my mind
I see you in anguished vision
with flowered wreath in hand
washed in a pallor of darkness
daubed and draped in tears
although my remains sealed and silent
now lie in endless sleep
my spirit free still roams the earth
outside the walls of death
and as it treads the church's aisle
it gently takes you by the hand
dries your sorrowed tears
and wipes your moistened cheeks
so if a warm embrace you feel
a tender transient touch
do not be afraid my dear
it is only me
still holding you in love
from death beyond the grave.

I DREAM OF OUR TIME OF TOGETHERNESS

The flowers you placed on my grave have long withered
no one visits this place anymore
I now know you belong to another
no more do I dwell in your heart.

Still as I rest in my slumber
submerged in the waters of Lethe
I dream of our time of togetherness
and a past that will never return.

If when you walk this garden path
you think of me and see me not
lay down yourself in sleep
and
dream me
then in your placid slumber
thread a silent prayer
that I may again one day awake
and
face the rising sun.

THE COLOUR OF MOURNING

After your departure
the colour of mourning stayed
infiltrating my marrow
furrowing my mind
serrating my heart.

The hour glass of time
erodes my living days
and I lament
that all I could have told you
will now remain unsaid.

Soon shall come the time when I am gone
then in the fullness of no time
I shall understand
that to live in the memory of those I have loved
is
not to die.

REMIND ME

Lost angel of my love
I endeavour to recall
why we parted long ago
time has fogged the chambers of my mind
in an unremembered past.

Now as I breathe my final breath
and
once more I hold your hand
I beg you dear
remind me
how did it end
did I lose you
or
refuse you?

WHEN I AM GONE

When I am gone
in the afterglow of time
I shall never love again
but
if you dream me in your dreams
the gelid fires of my heart
shall ignite again once more
rekindled by the sparkle
of your reverie of love.

DO NOT ERECT A TOMBSTONE

Do not erect a tombstone
to mark my mortal death
plant instead a cornfield
and
when the sun is at noontide
at the equinox of spring
ask your guardian angel
to let you borrow his wings
then from that apex in heaven
drop your palette of passion
on this elegiac canvas of rest.

The wheatfield now is ignited
my tomb a gravestone of gold
and
in the glow of this becoming
I dance in my garden of death.

WINTER IS HERE

Winter is here in twilights of cindered ashes
hours weave colours of fallen leaves
as trees bare limbs and flowers fade
days extend their shortest span
in straw-gray patterns of illusion
haunting symbols of man's transient life.

But Spring will come again
in ardent flames of blossomed joy
while branches reach the sky
ignite the fires of the sun
in surging songs of hope
vibrant echoes of time's eternal youth.

DO NOT CANDLES BURN

Adjacent to my life-less frame
when twilight falls and daylight dims
do not candles burn
expose instead my carcass to the night
and light up two or three of the billions
of the silent stars above
then let their twinkling light
steer me past this tortured path
and guide my weary wandering soul
to the promised land of hope.

But should this eclipsed alley
be still too dark to tread
I shall ignite in memory
the sparkle in your eyes
this beacon from my life-time
rekindled beyond time
will dance me through this threshold
to my treasured sacred home.

WAS IT YOU?

Was it you
who in that crowd did catch my eye
with glacial glance and gelid gaze?

Was it you
who later on that moonless night
lured me through the shadowed streets
of that town I love so well?

Was it you
who drew me near
then took my hand
and in the darkness of the night
placed a kiss upon my lips?

Then as entwined we traced
the city's criss-crossed alley ways
I saw the shadows at our feet
mine umbrageous black
yours albescent white
and as the dead no shadows cast
it was then I knew
that this indeed was you
returned in transient passage
from the sleep that knows no end
to bid your last farewell.

I TOO HAVE WEPT FOR LOVE

Along a road
layered and paved in ochre stone
on a day the sun set fire
to a field of wheat
before the evening twilight
we once walked together
your hands in mine
youth's ecstasy in our flaming hearts
I loved you then but know not why.

Now only a memory
blossoming in loneliness
on the horizon of my tangled thoughts
I yearn to walk that path again
and trace its muted auburn ways
words no longer shared
laughter lapsed into tears
youth's desire turned to broken dreams
I too have wept for love.

REACH OUT

Today
in tarnished waters
along the streets of this once golden place
the leaves have fallen
this ancient dying land
ochre-coloured in autumn tints
echoes fragments of time-worn gods.

Tomorrow
no more fallen petals
no shadows on these stones
no empty mirrors in the dust
the birds shall fly in joy
seek branches in the sky
in a new springtime of desire.

Reach out
touch the mountains of this sky
stand among the ruins of this land
a testament to the coming dawn.

In the eventide of life
I wanderer of oblivion
call your name once more
across the then and the now
that only time divides
although I have run my clocks backward
in the immeasurable distance of yearning
time has continued to pass
and now I aged and withered
am still awaiting your return.

Over the reddening theme of life
the days pass by
on clouds of many years.

The patterns of my love
like flowers in the wind
spiral in the scattered dust.

I see the sunlight in your eyes
eternal flower of my life
you draw and colour all my springs.

Mist has fogged these once bright threads
our rivers turned to mud
turgid tearful tides.

But times will change again
the unmade paths of life
shall slip away their masks.

Come walk along with me
with fire in your heart
and laughter on your face
through fields of summer landscapes
towards golden blossomed lights
to times beyond our own.

LOVE BETRAYED

You no longer come to my dreams
to find you
I must traverse the mirrors of incest
and visit another one's dream
your absence is telling me
what your words have failed to say
love is now betrayed.

THE LAST POEM

Now that I have lost my love for you
I ask the wind to float the music of your voice
on the lavendered clouds
of the savannah skies of eventide.

Then
as this airborne melody
is carried back to me
I take these returned echoes to weave them into words
and
from their latent alphabet
carve this poem
the last I shall ever write for you.

DO I NEED TO BE A POET

Do I need to be a poet
to ask the angels
to bridge the distance of our love.

No I do not need to be a poet
for the road map of our love
encompasses no longitudes or latitudes
no hereness or thereness
no near or far apart.

For me and you
under the sun
there is
no border or boundary
no measure of distance
no such place as far away.

I reach out to grasp the sounds around me
to smell the air
to feel the earth
to see the sky
to love and embrace life.

But all around me
turn their face
and I am left
forlorn
unfriended
lonely
in grey-walled grief
homeless in my own home
in a life that has no meaning.

An iceberg melting away
pouring love with no return
faced only by hostility
chiseled
clawed
strangled
fragment after fragment
till none remains
the silence of death delivers all.

I long to walk the laughing lanes
outside the walls of time
sanctified by silence
in a world of infinite dimensions
where love will reign supreme.

SUMMERTIME

Summertime
it is evening
the anguished sun descends
the harvest moon rises
stars light the azure skies
we hold hands
the seductive cathedrals of love
bloom in this moon beamed garden
we rise to celestial music
stand on pedestals divine
sing to a sleepless night
our echoed desires rise to the heavens
luminous passions unlocked
overcome with this pollen of plentitude
we die of an overdose of love.

Come walk with me
in a desert melting into infinity
through alabaster halls of silence
where our fertile oceans of happiness
born from origins secret and unknown
become but the sterile shadows of frozen music
as we turn into marble statues
our wounded hearts still shed human blood
spilled over bleached ashes of ancient wisdom
in the lost passageways of time.

Come descend with me
down saline stairs of oscillating moon-lit tides
through corridors embalmed with sadnesses unborn
deep into the petrified bowels of a subterranean sea
where avenues of vultures await our death
and poisoned webs of ancestral spectral doom
coagulate the cryptic crystals of our merging blood
here the ardent pillars of fire burn no more
in the long unending slumber
of a citadel of the dead.

Come rise with me
on sibilant waters of quiescent memories
through perfumed cascades of burnt galactic legends
to wash the sea with molten love
to nail our bodies to the clouds
to reach the heaven of our skies
and cast an endless ectoplasmic spell
illuminating the lost dark side of the moon
with the unquenchable white light of radiant hope
in an eternal incantation of our unconsummated love.

WHY?

Why is it that I am eternally going somewhere
and
constantly getting nowhere?

MY MIRROR WEPT

My mirror wept
when it no longer reflected my image
the reason it said
was
that
I was tired of being myself.

IN SEARCH OF MY REAL SELF

I walked through the plane of my mirror
to the realm of reflections reversed
then turned back to glance at the looking glass
to look my real self in the face
only sadly to discover
that now there was nobody there.

MY REFLECTED SELF

The mirror opens its portals
invites me to enter its vaults
I cross its membranes of silver
to walk the thresholds of awe.

On this other side of reality
I merge into the image
and
become my reflected self.

IT'S MAGIC

Why is it that a black seed
planted in a brown earth
turns into a green plant
which becomes a red rose?

I do not really want to know
I would rather still believe
it's magic.

IN BETWEEN

The
space-time
in
between
life and death
is
where and when
I
live my life.

What I still seek to find
is the space-time
in
between that between.

COULD SOMEONE TEACH ME

Could someone teach me
to measure
the perfume of a rose
the age of the wind
the height of the sky
the colour of poetry
the intensity of love?

THE NOTHING THAT I AM

God hung a picture in the sky
on the canvas of the heavens
and cast celestial patterns
to map the music of the spheres.

As I hold my breath in awe
and gaze upon this astral art
time passes to timelessness
and
I become aware
of
the nothing that I am.

I HAD LIVED IN TOTAL LIGHT

My shadow keeps changing its position
sometimes it is ahead of me
sometimes behind me.

Yesterday at noontide it stood under my heel
imprisoned between earth and the mighty sun above
my orphaned soul paled at this act of separation.

As its darkness returned anew
too late I become aware
that for an instant in my life I had lived in total light.

CIRCUMFERENCE OF MY TOMORROW

Today
I am concerned
about calculating
the circumference
of my tomorrow.

Tomorrow
I shall find
the future
tenaciously
outmeasuring
the widest compass
of my estimation.

THE SONG IN THE SKY

It is morning
in the citadel of the immortals
oceans of tragedy
nail my body to the sky
my spirit rides an airborne cloud
I open my mouth and swallow a star
the light of its opalescence
forms a rainbow in my heart
and
illumed with incantation
I become the song in the sky.

I fly the gryphon of wantonness
over the valley of Voe
to the cave of the magic maiden
on the isle of the mensural sea.

In this Arcadian wonderland
sorceress turns seductress
and
I diviner of ecstasy
walk a chimerical path
to share at the end of the rainbow
her erotic kingdom of lust.

On the other side of this poem
I have forgotten laughter
my sadness moonburned in odours of sorrow
in the landscapes of my mind
in the nevernoons of midnight
in times not measured by the clock
shadows scorch the cleavage of the skies
in sounds I cannot write
wounded flowers of the sun
weeping heaven's eyes
tears of stone
altars of pain
love misspelled.

On this side of the poem
I am no longer what I was
I come from the darkness
borne by gods unknown
in a dream flown by angels
my heart is on high
and
rising.

ECHO

As
ECHO
wept pined
and
withered
NARCISSUS
reflected

ECHO

Unable to voice
the music in my heart
in oral form
or carve my flames
in aural terms
I plead in muted silence
the last desire
of my living time.

Dreamer of illusion
take me in your arms
grant me the ecstasy of a parting kiss.

With dying wish declined
my body shrivels
my shadow fades
deliverance of desire
only comes in death.

Destined to division
in our lives on earth
in death once more apart
our spirits roam in separate realms
yours in Stygian waters
mine in Elysian halls.

But my consuming passion
lives on beyond my death
to now reword in echoed tones
what many times it yearned to say
and could not tell you then
Narcissus
I love you.

As he walks the forest paths
a youth resplendent and sublime
fatigued from hunt he pauses
to rest his virgin frame
as he stoops to quench his thirst
on the canvas of the lake
a vision he beholds
of skies and clouds and forest trees
and midway in this aqueous frame
an aquatint of splendour
the image of a youth
a mirror of perfection.

Now rested and restored
he reaches out his hand
desirous to possess
the visioned image
he is not aware is him
and as he taints the waters
which now reflect no more
the water song is silenced
the vision no longer there.

Then as the ripples dwindle
and the lake reflects again
beheld invites beholder
the seen becomes the seeing
the mirrored dream returns.

But he who loves his image
with unconsummated love
can take the pain no more
anguished and despondent
weary and forlorn
lays down his mortal body
to take its final sleep.

The waters now in sorrow
turn turgid and opaque
and on their curdled surface
stir his lifeless body
to distant Stygian shores
as mournful sirens pine
nymphs a requiem chant
for him by water sired
to water-grave returned.

Then the weeping heavens
bathe the coasting corpse
and as this love-smelt tincture
dissolves into the lake
a fresh and fragrant blossom
sees the light of day
a legacy bequeathed
by one whose fate it was
to love his mirror image
a fair and radiant flower
to which he gave his name.

She
a nymph of the forest
of beauty uncompared
too soon in nuptial union
condemned by Stygian spirits
to the dungeons of the dark.

He
a poet of the lyre
of vocal tone sublime
when florid strains he sang
the rapture of his song
even nature did disarm.

Agonised and anguished
at the taking of his spouse
a luring chant he pines
for the loved one he had lost
then no longer able
to bear this parting pain
he trails the tracts of Hades
imploring her return
his canticle of craving
a poem more powerful than a prayer.

The radiance of his song
illumes this penal realm
the music thaws the furnace
of the anguish of the damned
and as once more his prayer he tones
the judges of the dead
assenting to his plea
allow their captive free.

"Back to the realm of the living
she may indeed return
but as you lead her homeward
cast not your glance on her
when the rays of sunlight
caress once more her face
only then may you behold
the beauty of your bride."

As he starts his journey
straddling the ascent
through arduous rite and passage
towards xanthic noontide light
she in darkness follows
his lyred treble tone
and as they neared the sunlight
it seemed that love had won.

But doubting Stygian covenant
and unable to delay
he turns to set his gaze
on her fair and fragrant frame
his eyes her fleeting vision
for an instant did behold
then in pain and sorrow
he watched her slip away
and all too well he knew
that he again had lost her
this time forever more.

The song now is extinguished
the dulcet tones are mute.

Magician of the Muses
where is your music now?

THIRA

From the orifice of earth's menstrual flow
the land unfurled its scalding heat
shivered in orgasmic shakes
unleashed ignited hatreds of subterranean wrath.

Embryos of ash and bone
auras of darkness in poisoned winds
curdled blood in acrid moulds
cosmic arsenals of apocalyptic doom.

In this ashen dance of death
the earth that day for once lit up the sky.

PARADISE

Between
memory and oblivion
remembrance and desire
the not yet and the no longer
man
dreams of paradise
because
he lost it.

CAIN

Down in the valley
bent double
Cain tiller of the earth
in scorching heat
works at his patch of soil.

Up in the hills
seated
Abel keeper of sheep
in cool mountain air
trills at his flute.

Cain in envy listens
the music stings his heart
he pauses to relish his toil
wipes his weary brow
the sheep have trampled his crops
anger fills his soul
raising his stone carved hoe
fast and furious he hastens to the hills
... all too soon
the flute is silenced
and
tiller to killer
transmutes.

In the streets of Nod
assailed by assassins
Cain felt no fear at all
as he was protected by the mark of God
so he stood in confidence
and
looked them in the eye
then
distrusting Divine covenant
in dubiety he turned
... and saw the mark had gone.

ANGEL

Angel
you told me
about the beginning
an immaculate conception
a bloodless virgin birth.

Angel
why did you not also tell me
about the end
an ignoble crucifixion
a gory bloodstained death?

Angel
did you think
that if you had told me
my Son would not have died
and still redeemed the world?

OF THESE HE DID NOT SPEAK

After announcing to the Virgin
the immaculate conception
and
the bloodless birth
the Angel wept
for although he knew too well
about
the
passion
and
the
death
of these he did not speak.

The Son of Man is dead
for three days
His scarred and lifeless body
lay torpid in the tomb
then
as the sun rose on the third day
His body stirred
and
He
awoke
to
announce to the world
"I am the resurrection".

I AM THE RESURRECTION

Betrayed by a kiss in a garden
nailed to a cross on a hill
laid to rest in a tomb
the Son of God is dead
murdered by mankind.

There is a silence on the earth
there is a stillness in the air
the world is mute with grief.

For three days He slept in paradise
before rising from the dead
proclaiming
"I am the resurrection
he who believes in Me shall be redeemed".

THE HUMAN HEART

The
human heart
the
menotrome of life
whose mirrored motions
mark man's destined time.

When its clocktime cadence
ends its rhythmic beat
our borrowed stay concludes

ALL THIS HAD TO PASS

Over a hill of death
at the foot of a cross
a weeping mother
anguished and in tears
falls on bended knee
heartbroken and forlorn
looks up to her dying Son
scourged crucified
battered and bleeding
sees His blood drip down
and stain her vestal robes.

In these His final moments
He yearns to touch her face
and dry her mournful tears
though His human hands are nailed
His divine embrace she feels
and at the instant of His death
her eyes meet His
then illumed with divine wisdom
she understands too well
that for the scriptures to be fulfilled
all this had to pass.

THE BEGINNING

As God pondered on the design of the universe
He posed Himself this question
should the beginning be in numbers
or
should it be in words?.

THE LORD IS THERE TO TAKE HIS HAND

Through empty silent streets
in the shadowed light of dawn
the sound of hurried steps
disturbs the village sleep
a black clad priest
stole round collared neck
from church to house
transports the Eucharistic Host.

Through open door
up winding steps
to dim-lit attic walls
a near-death prayful corpse
on tarnished sheets of white
receives the blessed bread
then exhausted but fulfilled
departs this life in peace.

Convinced that as he tracks his path beyond this gate
The Lord is there to take his hand.

IN COMPANIONSHIP OF LONELINESS

In companionship of loneliness
through the stone walled streets
of a cube-house town
its profile straddled and sprawled
on fossil shoulders of a hill-top crest
decapitated by nature's force
I walk resigned
to the silence of a sheltered shrine
onyx lined and marble faced.

As there in pious prayer
I kneel in contemplation
in my quest for truth
from a votive hanging cross
a luminance I barely knew
emerges as a beacon guide
takes me to my final goal
and helps me reach my sacred prize
a dwelling in eternal light.

KLEPSYDRA

Over
the sea of knowledge
between
Harmonia and Helikondia
in mirrored chronometry
lies
Klepsydra
the land of the reversal of time.

There
arrival is departure
before is after
and
tomorrows are but yesterdays.

Here
where calendars run backwards
and
the sands of the hour glass rise
you need to be a mathemagician
to find your cadastral position
in this inverted dimension of time.

EUPHONIA

In the midst
of
somewhere and nowhere
near
Eudoxia and Eusapia
between
the valley of sound
and
the vale of silence
outside the range of the compass
without
latitude and longitude
lies
Euphonia
the citadel of music
sculpted in harmony
and
layered in tone.

When you walk this city of sonance
all is modelled in chant
a cadence more precious than silver
a canticle rarer than gold.

I DREAM A LAND

I dream a land as far away as freedom
perched on a mystic threshold of existence
where the ancient lamps of wisdom
are still the sacred writings of today.

I crossed the whirlpool of fantasy
to reach the shorelines of myth
there I met the incantatory unicorn
and asked him to tell me his tale.

"I belong to the ladders of legend
a creature of magic and myth
born in the onyxed mirror
a fanciful being of time.

I remember my life in the no time
in the vales and valleys of lore
before man learnt to want only evil
and forgot to love what was good.

Then God in an outburst of anger
sent a flood on the face of the earth
for all the planet to perish
save Noah the son of Lamech
for he and his family were righteous
in the judgemental eyes of the Lord.

From God's own divine blueprints
out of cedar he fashioned an ark
for himself and all of his kindred
and a pair of each creature on earth
so their lineage would continue to flourish
after the punitive waters withdrew.

At the time set for boarding
each creature lined up with its mate
then it seems in the chaos of loading
that Noah forgot me ashore.

The doors of the heavens then opened
the waters engulfed the whole earth
I wept as the rivers kept rising
and pined as the ark sailed away.

For many a day did I struggle
opposing the fierce raging storm
when all around me were drowning
and no living creature remained
my spirit exhausted extinguished
my species thus rendered extinct.

I did not live to see the rainbow
or the branch bearing dove of peace
the earth returned to green pastures
nor the glow of the resurgent light.

Now that I am no longer living
I really have no regret
the world through its history has taught me
it is better to live in a fable
than in the turgid reality of doom".

RAINBOW

After the flood
God put a rainbow in the sky
and
as this airborne music carves its crescent curves
I poet astonished and awed
in vain struggle to translate
this mystic code of colours
into a lyrical poem of words.

SUNFLOWER

Autumn
the sunflower is dropping its seeds
it is weeping its body away
age wets its dryness with sorrow
the gates of its splendour now closed.

Spring
the light of the flower returns
in the palm of its petals
imploding with gold
the handprint of God.

INVITATION TO A DREAM

I poet am a dreamer
who invites you to visit his realm
for only in the waters of dreamland
can I regale in the warmth of your arms
dreamscapes carved into lovescapes
on the slivered mirrors of sleep.

Then in the glow of the morning
as the poet gently awakes
the reverie wanes into absence
yet in the heart of the dreamer
the dream lingers on evermore.

THE BEGINNING OF WHAT I AM

Under the emerald face of the moon
I walk the chartless streets of delusion
cosmic mistress of the heavens
daughter of the fallen angel
I ask you the unanswerable question
what is the origin of life?

I rise from this dreamtime of shadows
to walk the songlines of truth
as I cross this threshold of sapience
my knowledge deepens
and
I comprehend
the beginning of what I am.

THE POWER OF DREAM

Nameless lover of my reverie
I write you my letters of longing
in verses of lyrical score.

The prose then dreams it is poetry
and dances out of the dream
lifts itself from its pages
and flies in the realm of the muse.

From this airborne poem
afloat in the mansions of sleep
a virtual petal of passion
drops down on a fallow field.

As vision transmutes to reality
a flower springs forth from the seed
a paean to the power of dream.

THE POEM REMAINS

Are you ghost
or
are you angel?

Spectral vision of the night
come forth from the darkness
bearer of the wisdom of the ancients
carried on the plumage of birds now extinct
hand me the book never written
bequeath me the text never read.

Voyager of the black midnight
lend me your wings plumed and feathered
let me fly the tightrope of knowledge
let me drink from the flagon of lore.

Clairvoyant tablets of culture
touchstones amont to our time
author long lost in oblivion
words preserved to this day.

The paradigm pattern continues
the poet passes
the poem remains.

Between
yes and no
now and never
the not yet and the no longer
lies
the crossroad of destiny.

THE ATHEIST CREED

In the nebulous mansions of afterlife
the only season is now
from this infinite dimension
there is nowhere to go.

Eternal centuries of nothingness
a diaphanous silence of nought
a vacuous tedium of sameness
even dreams have been taken away.

This is the neverness of always
an endless absence of time.

LOVE WAS BORN AGAIN

As she retraced
fragments of delight
retrieved from secreted memories
her heart froze
her blood coagulated
and
anticipating expectant futures
her love was born again.

THE UNWRITTEN POEM

When I was born
my mother died
her life exchanged for mine
although since then
time has spun a life long loom
for this son unknown to his mother
unable still to bide his grief
these tangled verses remain
a poem too painful to pen.

THE FOREVER UNKNOWN

I tread the paths of this city
to move on backward in time
on arrival I find I am leaving
events here happen before they occur.

All that has already happened
and that which still has to come
is recorded in the reflective mirrors
of the timeless tablets of now.

Only that which could or might have been
the if only perhaps and maybe
dance together in tandem
and remain forever unknown.

I forget what I don't remember
I remember what I don't forget
the less you remember
the more you forget
the less you forget
the more you remember
without forgetting
there would be no happiness
without remembering
there would be no sorrow
in balancing the two lies the secret.

IN SEARCH OF A DREAM

In search of a dream
I walk out of my sleep
across the drawbridge of consciousness
where time is no longer my prison
and
space renders me free.

In this trance of awakeness
I drink the wine of mantology
from the vine of the elsewhere of here
in this intoxicated reverie
I savour the palette of prophecy
and
witness my past and my future
in
an eternal instant of now.

WHEN DAY MEETS NIGHT

As day departs in a multi-coloured symphony
and night emerges in pallid tones of grey
the sanguine disc of a descending sun
joins
the argent circle of a rising moon
at this moment night and day are one
and
as I gaze on this frozen fugue of time
I am chastened and renewed.

THE FLOW OF TIME

As I walk these hand-toiled fields
the sun pours down like honey
a lazy lizard on a crumbling rubble wall
runs up in careless want
to sap day's dying rays
its rude ascent disturbs the calm
and
as if to mark the flow of time
in transient passage
a slithering stone descends.

IT IS ONLY THE BEGINNING

In this miracle
where horizons have no end
I poet and sage swim in ecstasy
in a sea once called tranquillity
with faith sublime
magical and blessed
I play darkness against light
resonance against resonance
moonkissed by the ghosts of eventide
I invite the stars to dance
in this hypnotic trance
I know nothing ends
it is only the beginning.

I WALK THIS LONELY ROAD

From nowhere did I come
to nowhere I shall go
in
between
I tread the pathways of my life
all that I am and shall become.

With no beginning and no end
I walk this lonely road
before I was I am already gone
in an existence
where nothing really is
but only seems to be.

AS WE COME TOGETHER

As we part
the ashen tones of absence
shadow my soul.

Then as we come together
the radiant light of your presence
illuminates my life.

THE WARMTH OF HER SMILE

The warmth of her smile
moistened
the
mirror.

The contours of her body
clouded
the
reflection.

The power of her love
cracked
the
glass.

Dreams they tell me
do not lie
now
I
know
why
no one
today
dreams
wisdom
anymore.

ONLY IN DREAMS

Although your love has called me back
from the looking glass of death
I know too well
that
only in dreams
do the living meet the dead.

In an afterlife untold
through eternal times of now
never again shall we share
the scriptures of our past
numinous epiphanies
aborted
in the waning moments
of this dreamless sleep.

AND WE SHALL MEET AGAIN

In the silence of the nights of no dream
I step out of my sleep
in search of reveries
to once more walk with you.

Since you have gone
I scan landscapes and seascapes
in search of the reincarnated stardust
of our lost world of lovescapes.

In a pain more powerful than time can heal
I eternal optimist still believe
that the dead will reawaken
and we shall meet again.

THE FUTURE IS NO MORE

Once there was a time
when my eyes shed no tears
and the chambers of my heart
ablaze in lambent glow
danced intoxicated in wines of delight
lavishing youth's lucent lovescapes
time future casting luring spells
of aureate hope and golden dreams.

Today I walk alone
on lonesome paths of sanguine shores
my life a cradle of anguish
woven on tangled looms of sadness
in the broken quicksilver
of non-reflective mirrors.

At this my journey's end
too late I understand
time has been my prison
and the future is no more.

Walk past the topaz doorway
and
climb the opal ladder
then cross the rainbow bridge
tread through the xanthic shore-line
to reach your onyx goal
a radiant golden garden
fashioned by the gods
then at its argent portals
these words in feathered plumes.

DESTINATION UNREACHABLE

Now many may not know this
but
once I roamed this place
as to how I got there
that secret stays with me.

A NEW DAY IS BORN

The crescent moon descends
the night yields its darkness
washed in ablutions of dawn
light bathes the heavens
the sun is ignited
a new day is born.

NIGHT CALLS IT A DAY

The
threshold
between
darkness and light
is
crossed
and
as
the
sun rises
night calls it a day.

LIGHT RETURNS AGAIN

The sky falls out
in the silence of this wound
birds no longer fly
rain no longer falls
who will light the moon?
who will dance the stars?

In anvil voice
a flash of thunder
ignites the night
cuts through the sable tones
and
light returns again.

PAST THE PORTALS OF PARADISE

At the crossroads of my after-life
in labyrinthine spirals of the here-after
the compass of my soul steers me
through sunless passageways of timelessness
to the unchannelled choreographies of endlessness.

Past the portals of paradise
this darkness dissolves into light
and
I emerge transfigured
in the constellated epiphany of eternity.

YESTERDAYS RECALLED

In an instant past and present bridged
on the ceiling of the rainbow of now
mirrored recollections of yesterdays recalled
relived
retold
recorded from the past
reminiscences not erased
ancient times retrieved
enriched
enhanced
enraptured and endowed
by the memory of you.

YOU CALL ME BACK

I am wounded
the sky pales at my sorrow
lost in darkness
I fashion my prayer.

Search me
reach me
find me.

You call me back
I rise again
anointed and blessed
I know I am yours again.

As you trace my skin
flower of my desire
I lip read your touch
rhythms on my flesh
tactile music
silent chords
mantras
unheard unseen
love letters
scripted
read
and
understood.

Between now and then
and here and there
our paths once crossed
but our lives went different ways
yet in that moment all too short
a love was born.

Although years have passed
and youth has flown away
I know the day will come
when
somewhere sometime
between here and now
and
there and then
midway in some galactic space of time
we shall meet again
and
walk a common path.

AND WE AWAKE IN PARADISE

Let us go, you and I
and steal some sand from the hour glass of time
to dream a dream of rest
then in that impossible wonder of silence
and naked tranquillity of calm
the dream transmutes
and we awake in paradise.

THE LOVE I HAD FOR YOU

My memory scans the past
listing my loves of yesterdays
balanced between fire and ice
now all lost in time.

Kaleidoscopic loves were these
washed with snow-flaked stars
fusions of illusions
to lacerate my soul
yet amongst them all a crystal casket shone
the love I had for you
luminous and numinous
sanctimonious
an alchemy of absolutes
that is what ours was.

MY DREAM LAST NIGHT

My dream last night
floated into a poem
then vanished into the land of forgetfulness
shadows of words unwritten
surrendered to silence
in the no time of never.

Flotsam from afar
in a night of sleepless quiver
overcast and grey
thoughts from a forgotten past
fleetingly returned.

Then
like fluvial waters
no sooner were they here
that they were gone forever
never to return.

THE FLOWER IN MY HAND

Sorceress of my life
although we parted long ago
last night we met again
in a dream you handed me a rose
when I awoke
by the quicksilver of magic
and the enigma of chance
I found a flower in my hand
petals of a dream
transumed to reality
your talisman of love.

NAMELESS LOVER OF MY HEART

In the silence of a night of a no dream
nameless lover of my heart
in vain I search for the verses
to write you a poem of love.

I scan the mansions of heaven
and beg the queen of the night
to lend me her moon-dust of magic
to lustre my songlines with light.

My incantatory plea is unanswered
my song remains unsung
my poem still-born and sterile
is drowned in its waters of birth.

A POET'S PASSING

When I die
no wreaths on my bier
no weeping at my grave
the only requiem a parting prayer
and the pealing
of death's doleful knell at a poet's passing.

IF BY CHANCE I'LL LIVE AGAIN

At the moment of my death
I'll lay down and dream
of things planned but left undone
and how these I'll carry out
if by chance I'll live again.

Now that I have returned from the dead
no longer in spirals do I roam
going and growing
in the ever-expanding curvations of life.

Now I walk in circles
in replayed repetition
going and coming
eternally tracing the recurring circuits of after-life.

MY SHADOW

Under the glare
of a noonday sun
my shadow held its breath
for just a bit too long
... and then blacked out.

THE ORCHESTRAS OF MY MIND

On distant shores of timelessness
the orchestras of my mind
once played music uncomposed
silent notes unscored
harmonic tones unsung.

Rising melodies
from the sanctuaries of dreams
now hushed and muted
and
alas no longer heard.

TRUTH HIT ME LAST NIGHT

Truth hit me last night
between
a dream of faith
and
a sleep of doubt.

Sleep on pretender
for once awake
you
return to reality
to lurk in the allurement of lies.

Poet
awake
write this poem
as if it were your last
a cherished prayer for freedom
from
the troubles of this life.

As
the words remain unwritten
and
the poem unread
poet you must now know
from
the tangible intangibles
of
your unanswered plea
that freedom lies
only
in
silence
in
forgetfulness
oblivion
and
void.

MEANDERS OF MAGIC

Ribbons of light
meanders of magic
waves fragmented and broken
surging and swelling in rhythmic cadence
on the incandescent canvas of a moonlit night.

This is the ocean's heartbeat
undulating ceaselessly in eternal time.

WE SHALL HAVE MET AND LOVED AGAIN

One day on some stone-walled country lane
a young man shall meet his love
and in that instant without time
with no future and no past
their hands will intertwine
then in that eternal now
when the sands of time stand still
we shall have met and loved again.

Paul Xuereb

This remarkable collection of verse written over a good number of years is the work of an artist whose main activity for decades has been the creation of images in the form of buildings, of drawings and paintings, of photographs. The buildings have not been just images, of course, but structures to be used. However like the many pure images Richard England has created, they were meant to be regarded as statements about the meaning of life, about the relations between man and man, between man and God, about the significance of beauty, physical and spiritual, in the life of man.

Unsurprisingly, therefore, England's poetry is also the work of an image maker, for whom verbal textures, verbal rhythms and the very shapes of his verse are as important as the often recondite ideas and the frequently ecstatic emotions he is striving to express. His writing is an endless struggle to achieve what can rarely be achieved: a perfect union between form and content. The glittering vocabulary he so often uses, from which rich and unfamiliar words drawn from many sources, including philosophy and esoteric religions, flash out intriguingly, reveals to the reader a poet who exults in the name of poet, a word he uses of himself again and again in this collection. Like some of the Romantics of the past, he is intoxicated by words, and stimulated by them to explore ideas for which a normal vocabulary cannot possibly be adequate.

"Sanctuaries: chronicles of solitary wanderings" can be viewed as a spiritual diary of a long pilgrimage, a journey in search of the author's identity and of his relations with both divine and human lovers. It is a pilgrimage that takes him at times to the limits of consciousness and of life itself, sometimes leaving him bewildered on the frontiers between the present and the future, or fascinated as he is transported to a future existence where the love he lost or never gained in this life will be for ever achieved.
Many of the poems reveal him as a profoundly religious person, a Christian who believes in man's redemption by God through His Son, even having a

strong feeling for the role of the Virgin Mary in the achievement of Christ's redeeming death, and above all, and passionately, in life everlasting beyond the grave. This belief in immortality adds a special dimension to a good many pieces in this collection, whether he is looking back at primitive man in Malta, thinking of a loved one long dead with whom he ardently hopes to be reunited in the next life, or just brooding over the day when it will be his turn to die. His Christianity does not deter him from exploring what other faiths, especially those of the Orient, have to teach about life and living.

Love and light are the two elements in his life that can raise him into ecstasy. Love is an experience that has formed his soul, and he often tries to recreate a far-off moment when love burgeoned, or tries to kindle a belief in a renewal of that love in another dimension. Light is nature's sculpting agency on earth, and thus an essential agent for the visual artist, but even when his medium is words, it is light that makes him intuit the mystic alliances between earth and what lies beyond it.

The picture he gives us again and again is that of an essentially solitary man, a being akin in spirit, if only to a point, to the Romantic artist of the 19th century. His solitariness, however, is that of the man who wishes to penetrate below the surface of life, who gazes at the universe and tries to tease a meaning out of it. He is no Childe Harold, no being under a curse to wander both in spirit and in space without ever making sense of things and ever feeling alienated from his fellows. Happiness may not come easily to him, but he is certainly no stranger to it, and the ecstatic moments he encapsulates so vividly in some of his poems testify to his ability to transcend the humdrum hours of life, to find a mystical unity between here and the beyond, in preparation for the moment when he will find himself in union with that beyond.

Of the 153 poems in this collection, there are many in which England has found the mood, the choice of words and imagery, and the rhythms that seize our imagination. Then there is a handful of pieces where his inspiration goes even further, and the verse makes us wonder at the experience he has consecrated in verbal pictures, making us sharers of the poetic moments that lie behind the verse.

The image of "drifting stage-sets of the mind" in his opening poem, "Dance of Dialogues", is one of those vivid pictures he can come up with. England has designed superb scenery for the stage and is one of the most knowledgeable people in this country about opera. Indeed, opera, with its magnification of emotions and its frequently exotic stage pictures marks more than one piece in this collection. If there are times when we feel overwhelmed by his vocabulary and by the cosmic imagery that comes so naturally to him, we are still grateful that there are still poets who have had enough of the earth-bound verse so many authors have been pouring out for decades.

The first poems are meditations on the distant past, on a Malta that was primitive save in its profound spirituality, a spirituality that can still inspire man in our own time. Some of them are love poems addressed to our island: "island cast in my prayers / island shaped in my fantasy / island fashioned in my thoughts." Perhaps the most arresting image of Malta is in "Stranger on Earth", where he describes it unforgettably as "Iceberg of stone / melting in a burning sea." This group of poems, some of which are among the finest in this collection, also includes a piece in which the author achieves full success by paring his language down to a minimum: "Island / carnage / tomb / the birds have gone."

The sense of loss he expresses in several poems is at its strongest in a group of poems about Gozo where he spent part of his childhood, a Gozitan childhood for which he feels strongly nostalgic. In one poem, "Għawdex", he tries again, and once more successfully, to create a poetic effect through sheer simplicity with a roll-call of Gozitan place-names; "Through Mġarr / Għajnsielem / Qala / and Nadur. / To Xagħra / Rabat / Kerċem /and Munxar. / Past Għarb / Għasri

/ Xewkija / and Sannat." Never has such a melody been made out of this island's place-names. In another, "Gozo", he uses very short verses to describe the colours of Gozo, almost like a pointillist painter, my favourite stanza being: "Streets ochre / salt-pans silver / sunsets gold." Among these colours he "once danced overdosed in the ecstasy of youth". Memory, which so many people lose in their old age, is a source of bitter-sweet emotions for him, a mixture of pleasure recalled and consciousness of a past that is for ever gone. A poem in the Gozo sequence, "Citadel", is noteworthy not just for its atmosphere and its dark sense of loss, but also for the pyramidal shape of the stanzas, which open up from a short statement establishing the physical environment, to a final 12 syllable line depicting his state of mind.

The many poems about old age, the end of life, and death range from a vaguely mawkish piece, "Your Last Farewell to Me", to dignified and restrained poems such as "The Winter of this Life", with its sombre closing words, "the winter of this life / descends too soon ahead of time." "The poem Do I Consume Time?" owes an unconcealed debt to Shakespeare's "I wasted time and now doth time waste me", but he is entirely himself in the closing lines in which we see death "spoilt for choice" waiting in ambush for him. In some pieces he broods about his own death and its imagined effect on his loved one, while in a chilling piece, "Was It You?", it is his love who comes back from the dead to haunt him with a gelid kiss.

Few poems in this collection are humorous in tone. One notable exception is "My Mirror Wept", in which the author laughs at himself, imagining that his mirror is no longer reflecting him, because, the mirror tells him, "I [i.e. the author] was tired of being myself." In a striking piece, "On this Side of the Poem", he actually comments on laughter and joy, saying, "On the other side of this poem / I have forgotten laughter", but counterbalances this with the verses, "On this side of the poem / I am no longer what I was... my heart is on high / and / rising."

His short "Echo" and "Narcissus" sequence contains beautifully crafted and often witty pieces. The second of his two poems entitled "Echo" may throw a light on eroticism in a Christian's life, "With dying wish declined / my body shrivels / my shadow fades / deliverance of desire / only comes in death." In a later poem, "My Reflected Self", he sees himself doing an Alice through the looking-glass act and becoming his "reflected self." Is this meant to be a postscript to his Narcissus poem?

The only purely narrative poem is a fine retelling of the Gozitan legend of St Dimitri, which vies with Guze Delia's classic version in Maltese verse. The short piece, "The Cave of the Magic Maiden", is in the spirit of Spenser's *Faerie Queen*, an attractive allegorical description of encounters with lust caused by a "sorceress turn[ed] seductress".

I have chosen just a few pieces to illustrate the range and stylistic ability of England's verse. I shall touch on just one more, to show how seriously he sees his role as a poet, and his longing for his work to survive him. In the spirit of Horace and Dun Karm, perhaps Malta's greatest poet so far, he pictures poets who are long dead while their work still lives to delight new generations of readers, his last words being a tribute to Dun Karm, whose famous lines in *Non Omnis Moriar* he anglicizes: "the poet passes / the poem remains."

NOTES

PAGES 16-37
The Maltese archipelago boasts a number of unique Neolithic structures that predate the great ancient monuments of Egypt and the Middle East. These remarkable architectural and engineering manifestations are the first examples of man's free-standing buildings created by a peace-loving civilisation which worshipped a deity of the earth and harboured a particular interest in the cyclic movement of time. These temples, whose people vanished into oblivion in the middle of the third millennium BC, are a remarkable testament of the lost knowledge, skills and qualities of ancient man.

PAGES 16-23, 69
The islet of *Filfla* is situated 5km south of Malta. Because of its cleft-shaped altar-table-like silhouette it was probably an important alignment reference for the Neolithic temple builders of Ħagar Qim and Mnajdra some 5000 years ago. For many centuries the islet housed a troglodyte chapel originally constructed in the 14ᵗʰ century. In more recent times it was used for target practice by French, Turkish, Italian, American and British forces. A local legend relates the creation of the isle; the inhabitants of one of the main island's coastal villages were so sinful that God caused an earthquake to destroy it, leaving a void depression known as *Il-Maqluba* on the outskirts of the village of Qrendi. The legend continues to narrate that the village was too evil even for the devil, who, in refusing it, hurled it skywards and on landing in the sea it formed the islet of *Filfla*.

PAGE 45
At the time when Gozo was subjected to pirate and corsair raids, a pious woman from the village of Għarb dedicated her only son to San Dimitri to ensure his lifelong protection. On one particular raid, the invaders seized the young boy and carried him away. Desolated, the woman ran to the cliff-edge chapel dedicated to the saint to implore his help. The legend recounts that the altar piece painting came to life and the horse-mounted San Dimitri galloped to the pirates' vessel and returned with her son. In gratitude, the woman vowed to keep the church oil lamp alight for the rest of her days. Years later the chapel was destroyed by an earthquake, its ruins descending on the nearby seabed. Later, in the 19ᵗʰ century, a ship seeking shelter from stormy seas adjacent to the chapel's former location, had difficulty drawing up anchor. A group of sailors descended to disentangle it. On their return they recounted that they had seen a chapel on the seabed and that they had walked into it where a painting of San Dimitri hung, illuminated by the flame of a still alight flickering oil lamp.

PAGE 52

Hwa om Sah (Buddha Field) in Jeonnan, South Korea is one of the outstanding Buddhist temples, founded in 544 AD by Yeon Gi, who, according to legend, travelled to Korea from India on a dragon-faced turtle. The site was visited by the author in 2005.

PAGE 106

Voe, a mythical exotic valley in L. Frank Baum's book *Dorothy and the Wizard in Oz.* Its inhabitants are invisible people.

PAGE 113

Thira or *Santorini* is the southernmost island of the Greek Cyclades. According to legend this was the location of the mythical city of Atlantis destroyed by the volcanic eruption of 1450 BC.

PAGE 128

Harmonia, Charles Fourier's imaginary group of colonies with a community life based on full freedom given to human passions.

Helikonda, one of the Isles of Wisdom in Alexander Moszkowski's 1922 story *Die Inseln der Weisheit*, where the main focus of the inhabitants is the unification of the arts.

Klepsydra, the sanitarium of the reversal of time created by Bruno Schulz in his *Sanitarium pod Klepsydra*.

PAGE 129

Euphonia, a city in Germany whose inhabitants do nothing but play or practise activities concerned with music, in composer Hector Berlioz's novel *Euphonie, ou la ville musicale. Nouvelle de l'Avenir.*

Eudoxia and *Eusapia*, two imaginary cities in Italo Calvino's *Invisible Cities.*

BIOGRAPHICAL NOTES

BRIAN J. DENDLE was born in Oxford, England, in 1936. He has BA and MA degrees from Oxford University and MA and PhD degrees from Princeton University in Romance Languages and Literatures. He was Professor of Spanish Literature at the University of Kentucky from 1971 to 2005. He was editor of *Romance Quarterly* from 1982 to 2002. He is the author of 14 books and over 150 articles on the modern literatures of Spain, France and the Mediterranean.

PAUL XUEREB. Born in Valletta, Malta, he is a graduate in law and English of the University of Malta, and was awarded a postgraduate diploma in library science by University College London. Between 1967 and 1997 he directed the University of Malta's libraries in which he introduced computerisation. He was a founder-member of the Malta Library Association (now the Malta Library and Information Association) in 1969, and he represented it at the founding meeting of the Commonwealth Library Association in 1972, an Association to which he was elected president from 1979 to 1983. He has been the chief theatre critic for *The Sunday Times* (Malta) since the early 1960s and sat on the Management Committee of the Manoel Theatre from 1992 till 2003. Since January 2005 he has been *Fondazzjoni Patrimonju Malti's* general editor and editor of the quarterly journal *Treasures of Malta.* He is currently Chairman of the British Culture Association. His publications include *Melitensia* (1974) *A bibliography of Maltese bibliographies* (1978), *Promoters of Information* (1990), *The Manoel Theatre: A short History* (1994), *The Maltese Opera Libretto* (2004?), articles on Maltese libraries in *Encyclopaedia of Library and Information Science* (1976) and in *World Encyclopaedia of Library and Information Science* (1993)

RICHARD ENGLAND was born in Malta and graduated in Architecture at the University of Malta. He continued his studies in Italy at the Milan Polytechnic and also worked as a student-architect in the studio of the Italian architect-designer Gio Ponti. He is also a poet, sculptor, photographer and artist. He is the author of several books on both art and architecture, and a number of monographs have been published on his work. Richard England holds professorships at various universities in the USA, UK and Europe. He is an Honorary Fellow of the American Institute of Architects, an Academician at the International Academy of Architecture and an Officer of The Order of Merit of the Government of Malta. His buildings and designs have earned him numerous international prizes and awards. Among his best known buildings in Malta are the Church of St Joseph at Manikata, the Central Bank of Malta Annexe, the

Millennium Chapel and the St James Cavalier Centre for Creativity in Valletta. Richard England has worked in the capacity of Architectural Consultant to governmental and private institutions in the following countries:- Yugoslavia, Saudi Arabia, Iraq, Italy, Argentina, Poland, Bulgaria, the ex-Soviet Union, Kazakhstan and his native Malta. *Sanctuaries* is Richard England's fourth book of poems.

JOHN HEJDUK (1929 - 2000) visionary architect and pedagogue, was for nearly three decades Dean of the Cooper Union School of Architecture in New York. Described as "the Architect who drew angels", Hejduk's allegorical creations in both theoretical architectural projects and haunting verse were embedded with an elegiac force of poetic exuberance. The letter reproduced on page 5 was sent to the author of "*Sanctuaries*" with a copy of Hejduk's 1998 book of poems "*Such Places as Memory*" and refers to Richard England's collection "*Eye to I*"

INDEX

INDEX OF DRAWINGS

The title of this collection, *Sanctuaries* was suggested by Brian J. Dendle.

Richard England's poems have been set to music by Charles Camilleri and
Marc England.

Sanctuaries is Richard England's fourth book of poems; *White is White*, an eulogy
on the colour white was published in 1973; *Island: a Poem for Seeing* in 1980;
and the collection *Eye to I* appeared in 1994.